The CONFIDENCE TALK

I SAID SOAR

IDARA INWEK OGUNSAJU

The Antorge Group LLC

Copyright 2023
Published by: Antorge Publishing
An imprint of The Antorge Group LLC, San Diego, CA
All Rights Reserved.

LIBRARY OF CONGRESS CATALOGING-IN-PUBLICATION DATA

Title:	The Confidence talk: I SAID SOAR
Author:	Idara Inwek Ogunsaju
ISBN (Paperback):	979-8-9853740-1-8
ISBN (EBook):	979-8-9853740-0-1
ISBN (Hardcover):	979-8-9853740-2-5

🌐 www.antorgegroup.com
📷 @Antorgegroup

The CONFIDENCE TALK

I SAID SOAR

IDARA INWEK OGUNSAJU

I SAID SOAR
The Confidence Talk

Dedication:

To Mom and Dad, Antonia and George, for whom
The Antorge Group is named. Thank you for creating a
home that allowed me to be seen, heard, and to feel
confident, even when I was far away.
This is for you.
Idara

Table of Contents

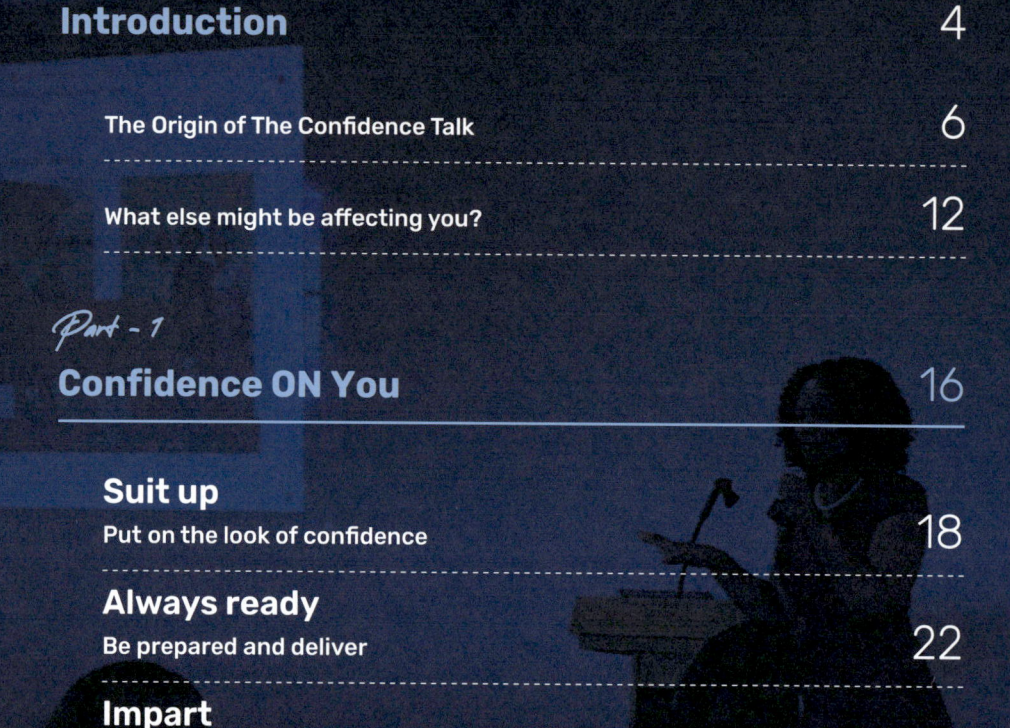

Introduction — 4

The Origin of The Confidence Talk — 6

What else might be affecting you? — 12

Part - 1
Confidence ON You — 16

Suit up
Put on the look of confidence — 18

Always ready
Be prepared and deliver — 22

Impart
Share your skills, talents, and Knowledge...to a diverse audience — 28

Don't spread your panic
My take on 'Fake it till you make it' — 35

## The BONUS section	40

Bonus 1: People are people	42

Bonus 2: It's not you and it's not just you	44

Part - 2
## Confidence IN You	52

Self-Regard
Know yourself. Like yourself	54

Offering
Do Good.	60

Advance
Keep Training	63

Recharge/Refuel
At the village or at the pump	68

## Conclusion	74

Introduction

I SAID SOAR
The Confidence Talk

Welcome.

I am glad you picked this book so we can talk about confidence.

They say absence makes the heart grow fonder. That is to say, you have a better appreciation for something when you are missing it, or when it's gone. The same can be said for confidence; you better appreciate the value and impact of confidence when you don't have it, or when your sense of confidence is low. That was my experience with confidence.

Some years ago, I thought nothing of feeling confident and in control; I simply went about my business. I did not have any reason to describe myself, but if you asked me, I would say I was confident. Then I went through a phase at work when my self-assuredness seemed to have gone missing. Not only was I feeling less confident than my usual self, I was also verbally expressing self-doubt. Sometimes without being asked. It was uncomfortable to be so uncertain where that had not previously been the case. Furthermore, my confidence in my own work also started to suffer. As someone who always took pride in the quality of my work, that was the tipping point. It became important to me to figure out how to regain my sense of self-confidence and to recover my footing at work.

This book is a compilation of the strategies I used to regain confidence. It also includes some lessons learned along the way. Even after a relatively short time of having lost confidence, it took practice and learning some new behaviors to feel confident again.

If your confidence has faltered, if you have started to persistently doubt yourself at work, this confidence talk is for you. My focus in this book is on you. There are a number of factors that can negatively impact your confidence, and the same factors will determine what steps you need to take to rebuild your confidence. This does not make what you are experiencing any less real. In fact, there's a whole section in this book to let you know it's not you and it's not just you.

I SAID SOAR
The Confidence Talk

However, my focus is first on your knowing that you are affected, and then taking steps to rebuild your confidence.

We will start with the outward-facing components that convey your skills and provide you with evidence of your ability and success. The second part of the talk is about feeling confident, building on your sense of self and knowing where to draw from for self-validation. In the bonus section, we will go over two messages. The first is recognizing that people are people – ultimately, we are all human. Then the second bonus *It's not you, and it's not just you*, is about recognizing the patterns in the workplace that can, and do, affect one's confidence.

The Origin of *The Confidence Talk*

I first shared The Confidence Talk with a group of young professionals in 2017. The talk consisted of the list of strategies I used to regain confidence in the workplace. I called it Be Still, The Confidence Talk. I loved the image that 'be still' conjured: one of certainty, control, and calm. "Be still" was also the first part of my favorite psalm and poem as a child (Psalm 46:10, The Holy Bible). The following year, I created a workbook based on The Confidence Talk©. When I launched The Antorge Group I used the workbook in small group sessions to guide the conversation as we went through the strategies. I considered making the content of the talk available to be used outside of the workshops and it was from that idea that this book was created. Next came a name-change for The Confidence Talk. A friend suggested creating an acronym that would make the components of the talk easier to remember. Not too long afterwards, I matched the strategies to the letters of an acronym - I SAID SOAR came to represent The Confidence Talk©. It is the same story, the same strategies, but easier to remember – I SAID SOAR.

I SAID SOAR
The Confidence Talk

The I in I SAID SOAR stands for me, and it stands for you. The rest of the acronym represents the strategies I used: **S**uit up, **A**lways ready, **I**mpart, **D**on't Spread your panic; **S**elf-regard, **O**ffering, **A**dvance, and **R**echarge/Refuel. I SAID SOAR conjures an image of an eagle, or a phoenix, soaring. In I SAID SOAR, I see elevation, calm, certainty, and control. I see confidence rising.

Merriam-Webster's dictionary defines confidence as a feeling or consciousness of one's own **powers** or of reliance on one's **circumstances**. Confidence is knowing your own powers or knowing that you can rely on your circumstances. This means that you can gain a sense of certainty from knowing what you are capable of and feeling that you are powerful. You also gain a sense of certainty from knowing or feeling that you can rely on who or what is around you. Conversely if you find your circumstances unreliable, or do not feel or believe in your own powers, your sense of certainty will be shaken.

While this talk is about you, the environment you are in is a major part of your work experience. Take note of when and where your confidence is negatively impacted. You will likely be applying the strategies from this talk for yourself in that environment or circumstance.

The confidence talk is focused primarily on the workplace. This was the setting for my own failing confidence. Oftentimes the tools and rules in the workplace are different and limited, relative to the tools you may use outside of the workplace. At work, you may second-guess a course of action for fear of jeopardizing your employment, while outside of work you may not have the same concern or need for restraint. The Confidence Talk© is simultaneously about the professional and the personal because when you are adversely affected at work, it can take a toll on your overall well-being. In discussing confidence, we tend to focus on self-confidence and place emphasis on the individual. The reality is that the people and culture around you can impact your sense of confidence tremendously. An unreliable or difficult work environment – even just one key relationship – can impact your sense of certainty and your ability to enjoy success in that setting. I SAID SOAR focuses on you, your sense of power, and your own influence to boost and rebuild your confidence.

I SAID SOAR
The Confidence Talk

To use an everyday analogy, let us imagine that you are walking and then you trip. If you stumble or lose your balance while walking, you reflexively catch yourself and then examine the ground. You may pause to check the area or keep walking with a brief glance back without losing time or face, in hopes of figuring out what made you trip. You may also keep checking the ground for a few steps to avoid another trip hazard before you feel comfortable enough to look ahead and continue walking without looking down. So it is with your confidence, you catch yourself and continue to move forward. Then, time permitting, you may assess what happened so that you can avoid it in the future. If it does not seem that serious you may hardly break a stride. In any case, you keep walking because you know how to walk, and you have places to go. The impact of tripping, figuratively, will not be the same for everyone. Loss of confidence can look and feel different for each person. The main thing is to catch it and address it. Pay attention to what is different for you, note changes in how you feel about yourself and your ability to perform successfully in the workplace. It was in noticing a change in how I felt that I first became aware that my confidence was not where it needed to be.

In retrospect, if I were to be asked what confidence felt like to me, I would say feeling confident meant being comfortable as myself no matter where I found myself. It meant stepping into a room or situation expecting to be successful and not unduly anxious about things I could not control. Confidence was being myself and accepting others as themselves. This attitude had always made me less likely to internalize another person's opinion or emotion. If, for example, I was working with someone who was expressing frustration about a change I was introducing to the workplace I would make a separation between myself and the frustration they were experiencing. Having that perspective, I could then have a direct conversation about the change that would put us on the same page. How confident I felt was directly impacting my sense of control and influence, and even my reactions to what people said or did. So, when I was not my usual confident self, the difference was clear to me. I was more likely to internalize reactions around me as though they were a reflection of me. I was also more likely to feel the need to prove my expertise and knowledge.

I SAID SOAR
The Confidence Talk

Loss of confidence resulted in my adopting placating behavior and keeping my professional opinion to myself in anticipation of it not being welcome. The irony is that being quiet when I had a different perspective to share was making things worse for my self-confidence. Placating or trying to downplay your effect can sometimes embolden the wrong behaviors in others. My placating and avoiding conflict did not improve working relationships. Instead, when, I allowed some boundaries to go unchecked self-doubt crept in and began to grow. I felt uncertain about things that I knew and could have done with ease. Feeling uncertain about these things, I started to seek validation excessively, to have someone check and agree that everything I was working on was good enough. At some point, I became embarrassed to even have these doubts and was determined to understand and address them for myself. I had felt the change in my confidence level before I became conscious of it and decided to do something about it.

Your confidence is worth protecting. Confidence not only gives you the power to be you but also to do every new thing before experience confirms that you can indeed do it. If you feel changes in your self-confidence, pause and take the time now to rebuild and bolster your confidence so that you do not lose your place or sense of self. Avoid expending too much energy in a defensive or reactive frame of mind – this can take some practice. Focus instead on what is most important to you and build on it. Focus on your goal and what will get you there. Later in this book under the topic of Advance, I go over focusing on goals and keeping your eye on the prize. Beyond just being successful on paper at work, the added benefit of being confident in yourself is being able to enjoy your successes. There was an urgency for me, a need to rebuild my confidence. As a result of this need to rebuild my confidence in the workplace, The Confidence Talk© was born.

The Confidence Talk© started out as a conversation. First within myself, identifying what I could do to regain self-confidence, then writing it all down as I implemented the effective strategies.

I SAID SOAR
The Confidence Talk

It was not too long afterwards that I shared the Confidence Talk© for the first time with a group of young professionals. I have since shared the confidence talk with various groups, particularly women in the workplace and in business. I shared the strategies I used to rebuild my confidence in two categories:

1. The confidence **ON** you – conveying confidence in the workplace
2. The confidence **IN** you - rebuilding your self-confidence and identifying tools for self-validation.

This approach was exactly what I needed. I wanted to exhibit confidence at work, I also needed to get back to feeling like my confident self internally. I needed both. And that is often the reality as you assess your circumstances, that there is still the work to be done and a career to maintain. So, the talk begins with maintaining those professional gains and influencing your work environment.

SAID:

Suit up, **A**lways ready, **I**mpart, and **D**on't spread your panic. This is the outward-facing and visible evidence of confidence at work. Your demonstrated skills and abilities along with the benefit of your experience. SAID is the part of your work that people see and experience.

SOAR:

Self-regard, **O**ffering, **A**dvance, and **R**echarge/Refuel. This part is about truly reconnecting with yourself and looking beyond your work identity. It is taking the time to focus on yourself – who you are, what you are capable of doing, your goals, your standards. It is also about taking the time to recharge and refuel in community and with the help of professionals as needed.

I SAID SOAR
The Confidence Talk

This two-pronged approach recognizes that there is self-confidence separate from being able to rely on your environment or circumstances. Let's start with your own definition of confidence.

What does confidence mean to you? How do you define confidence? Write down your own definition of confidence and some words and ideas that you associate with confidence.

What does Confidence mean?

I SAID SOAR
The Confidence Talk

What else might be affecting you?

Having captured your definition of confidence and words that describe what it means to you, it is important to note that what feels like the absence of self-confidence may be transient. A temporary feeling that is passing by or may be due to something specific but not necessarily a lack of self-confidence.

Here are six factors that may be affecting you and can be intermittent or temporary in nature if they are addressed in a timely manner.

1. Tiredness, Exhaustion:

We all need to rest to function at our best. There may be circumstances where it seems as though you are losing confidence, but it is a temporary response to being tired or even exhausted. In this case pausing to create or take an opportunity to properly rest will allow you to regain perspective. Rest and recover sufficiently, then you can properly assess what needs to be done. If, however, you find yourself consistently tired or unable to recover, then the tiredness or exhaustion is a signal from your body. It is important to take the time to understand what is affecting you in this way.

2. Demoralization:

You could be disheartened or demoralized in certain circumstances. And provided the source of demoralization is addressed, that too will be transient, and your self-confidence left intact. And yes, you can be a leader, you can have an important title, and still be demoralized or disheartened. As with so many other emotions it is important to recognize and address what you are experiencing. When you can pinpoint and understand or address the source of this feeling, it is less likely to have a lasting impact on your sense of self, or your sense of power. If you determine that your environment is not reliable, you can decide the appropriate action to be taken and again still have your confidence left intact.

3. Dissonance:

This refers to disharmony or incongruity. When there seems to be a disconnect between two sources of information. Basically, something does not quite match up or seem right. It could be a difference between what you are feeling or experiencing and what you are being told. A work example might be receiving great reviews and comments from a key decision maker or boss about how well you are doing and yet not getting the promotion that is befitting your level of performance when you apply for it. Another example could be that you are working with a person whose words and actions do not match, or someone you cannot rely on. Dissonance is enough to throw you off but may not impact your confidence. The main thing is to recognize it and address it. Even if the incongruity itself is not resolved, it is less likely to affect your sense of confidence if it is addressed in a timely manner.

4. Delay or Stalling:

This is when you have a decision to make, or you have already made the decision but find the necessary action difficult, so you choose to delay taking action. An example for me was having to set a boundary with a close colleague. I knew it was necessary, but it was not easy, so I delayed having the boundary-setting conversation. I was stalling as I nursed some disappointment. The reality was that I did not want to accept the change I knew was coming so I delayed having the conversation. Once the necessary action is taken and the new normal established, it becomes easier to move forward.

I SAID SOAR
The Confidence Talk

5. Stress:

Here I am referring to the unwelcome, sometimes overwhelming response to circumstances that we call stress as opposed to stress or tension that can be beneficial and results in growth. Each person's experience of stress can be different: what causes it, how it looks, and how we address it. It's not so much what is causing the stress that matters as the fact that something is causing stress. You can be confident yet stressed. If the source of stress is anticipated and temporary – like an audit at work, the impact is different and even manageable because it is expected and has an anticipated end. If the stress was unexpected or does not have a foreseeable end, the impact is likely to be more significant and you may require help with addressing it. Whether you are dealing with anticipated or unanticipated causes of stress, how you feel and how you respond to people and circumstances will be affected. Ultimately you want to address the source of stress with help as needed. In the meantime, it is important to identify ways to mitigate the impact of stress to minimize the physical, mental, or emotional strain you experience due to stress.

6. Time for change:

It may also be time for change. You may have outgrown the role or find limited opportunities for advancement in the organization. Whether you are looking for something more challenging, something better aligned with your goals, or an improvement in your work experience, you may be resisting the feeling that it is time to move on. Your sense of confidence is intact, but you feel you cannot rely on your environment or circumstances to provide the professional growth you desire. You may be at a point where you need to decide on the next step before your morale is negatively impacted.

I SAID SOAR
The Confidence Talk

There may be other factors that can impact your self-confidence and sense of certainty in the workplace. In each scenario it is important to pause and address any of those factors early so that they do not become more of an issue for you in the workplace and beyond.

Without further ado, let us begin The Confidence Talk©.

I SAID SOAR
The Confidence Talk

The Confidence ON You

The Confidence ON you is what people see and experience as you and your work. This is the "SAID" in I SAID SOAR. When people think of confidence, this is often what comes to mind – how confidence looks and sounds. Confidence On you matters in the sense that it signals your own power and influence. Think of it as external evidence of confidence. When rebuilding my confidence some of the quickest strategies were those in this category. Beginning with the confidence on me was a short cut to showing what was in the works internally.

SAID ~ Suit up, Always ready, Impart, and Don't spread your panic.

The confidence **ON** you is what people see and experience as **you** and **your work**. So, you suit up, you're always ready, impart your skills, and "Don't spread your panic". S.A.I.D. This is the confidence ON you.

Suit up
Put on the look of confidence.

When you think of how confidence looks, you probably picture a combination of posture and clothing that convey confidence. Clothes can boost your self-image. Power Suit. Heels. A Lucky Tie. A favorite dress. Clothes, accessories, and even mementos can be symbolic and empowering.

When my confidence took a blow and I found myself unsure of where I stood in my work environment, I made a conscious decision to "suit up". To put on the look of confidence. My "suit" would serve to continue to signal my power to myself and to others. It is sort of like Wonder Woman or any of the main characters in the typical superhero story. Their power or strength is not in the outfit they wear but when it is time for business, when the stakes are high, they put on their suit, the uniform that tells the public who they are. On certain days the suit was as much armor as it was a uniform. My suit was literally suits, specifically skirt suits, paired with high-heeled pumps. The look of the suits and the heels combined were my show of confidence. As a young girl I often designed the outfits I wanted to wear, including skirt suits I had seen on Princess Diana of Wales. Years later as a professional I started wearing suits again, usually with a distinctive, or unexpected detail. I would check the mirror one last time before

I SAID SOAR
The Confidence Talk

leaving the house – one last confirmation that I was properly suited up. The rest of the day would be focused on the work to be done. I knew I had the look of what I wanted to convey – confidence, grace, and power. I also wanted to wear my suit comfortably so I avoided anything that might make me even the least bit self-conscious once I had put it on. I wanted comfort and fit, no tugging, no adjusting – just good looks. Along with the suit and heels, I reflexively pulled myself tall when walking. As an aside, I also learned that the sound of my shoes announced my approach.

The suit was a visual and tangible reminder of my power and my successes. When my confidence sufficiently recovered, I was not as aware of my suit, posture and gait. I was not dependent on those suits to convey confidence. Choosing to "suit up" when I needed it helped me to tap into power and to reflect the image I had established for myself.

Key Confidence Point:

Put on what makes you feel confident and signals your power. You are guarding your own sense of power and accomplishment and when you feel it, it conveys in other ways.

Applying Suit Up:

Your suit may not be a suit at all. What you use to signal your power may be a different item, maybe even a routine like playing music before an important meeting.

I SAID SOAR
The Confidence Talk

First, what does confidence look like to you?

You are, without a doubt, the source and keeper of the skills and abilities that are integral to your professional success. Even so, a timely and tangible reminder helps. What are your suits? What are some of your go-to clothes or accessories that contribute to that boost of confidence and why? What helps to ground you when you need it?

Use the space below to write, draw, or attach an image of what confidence looks like to you. Include your go-to confidence-boosting item. Is it your hair, a piece of jewelry, high heels? Those are some of the more common examples I have heard during The Confidence Talk. What does confidence look like on you? What does it mean to you to suit up?

Include your suit or list of suits below:

I SAID SOAR
The Confidence Talk

The "suit up" image: Include below a picture of confidence.

A

Always Ready
Be prepared and deliver

 Ready: In a suitable state for an activity, action, or situation. Fully prepared.

Pause and breathe. Get ready. Like the moment before you go on stage, or before a big presentation. It's the moment before you dive into that big thing. Before you get to the wings, before you present, you want to be ready, so you prepare in advance. The more prepared you are, the better you feel in the moment before you go on stage. At work and in life, you are not always getting ready for a presentation or for the stage but there are smaller moments that also feel like getting ready for a performance. The idea of *'Always Ready'* is to be prepared, but not in a state of tense waiting. Always ready means being prepared, doing the things that allow you to feel confident in your work and ready to share it with others.

I SAID SOAR
The Confidence Talk

When my confidence was impacted, I felt unsure about how the work I was producing would be received. Eventually, I also started to feel unsure about the work itself. I asked for opinions and validation about my own content from more people than was necessary. As I started to focus on reclaiming the confidence I previously had, I found that I still spent more time viewing and reviewing content than I previously had. Although I should have been confident that any one mistake would not be the assessment of my performance and ability, I was not sure that was the case. Initially, it took more preparation and review to even feel comfortable with the final product. Gradually, my confidence in my output was restored. I was well-versed in the information and better prepared with each opportunity to share. The significance here is that I became more certain of my work. This in turn gave me a more objective perspective on feedback I received.

There are times when despite being ready, we can still be thrown off by the unexpected. It could be a question about information that you do not have, or an update that you had not received. Sometimes it could be someone challenging the information simply because they can. Whatever the case, it is easier to keep in perspective when you know your work.

Over time I found my pace – I stayed informed about the organization and industry; I was adept at internal communication, so I shared information and closed the communication loop as needed. In my role, I was responsible for a lot of people and I was also accountable to the top leadership of the organization. As I shared more about the great work being done by my teams, I met and interacted with more people within the organization and my work was spotlighted. I started to take note of the positive effect of my communication with my direct reports, peers, partners, and other leaders in the organization. This ties into the next point of the confidence talk, Impart, which involves diversifying your audience. When you are rebuilding your confidence, small wins can make a big difference. These small positive feedback loops also served as objective feedback about the work I was doing and became my measuring stick for how I went about my work.

I SAID SOAR
The Confidence Talk

Outside of meetings, always ready meant having access to the information I needed. I made sure to reference any dashboards, updates from leaders on my team, and relevant organizational updates. I had a sense of pride in being ready. I started to make my way from feeling like not knowing it all was a failure on my part to recognizing that I could find the information that I needed. If necessary, I could always come back at an agreed-upon time with the necessary information. What may have felt like failure was often not failure at all and if I did make a mistake, it simply did not define me. This is another way in which having objective criteria was helpful. I was slowly returning to being able to separate fact from projected emotions.

In meetings, *always ready* sometimes meant recognizing when the question being asked was not necessarily the right one for the audience. When presenting on a topic, if I was asked a question that was not appropriate or relevant, I could redirect the audience member by making a statement that was more consistent with my message. If timing was more of the issue with the question, I would offer the option of a follow-up afterwards to make better use of meeting time. Curiosity also goes a long way – I started to ask questions myself. Whether clarifying, confirming, or simply postponing, asking questions proved to be a beneficial tool in groups and meetings. As I adopted these practices, I started to enjoy communicating again, especially as I ventured beyond the routine at work.

And that brings us to what *always ready* may look like for you. You pride yourself in your ability to do great work. You know how to do the work and if you do not know the answer, you know where to find it. These logical and rational things are not at the front of your mind when you are not feeling confident. When you are not feeling confident, you are more likely to be sensitive to criticism or to treat subjective feedback as though it were law. This is the time to intentionally set yourself up for success. Part of rebuilding confidence is to be prepared with relevant work and skills. There's a saying that sums it up quite well, "if you stay ready, you don't have to get ready".

I SAID SOAR
The Confidence Talk

Key Confidence Point:

Stay ready. If you stay ready, you don't have to get ready. Let the quality of your body of work speak for itself but let it also speak to you. Take pride in your work and build on your strengths.

Applying Always Ready:

Do you feel prepared to deliver on the primary expectations for your role? Are you using your strengths regularly in the course of your work? If you cannot confidently answer yes to these two questions, pause and apply this exercise:

First: What primary expectation do you need to work on, and what does being prepared in that area of work look like? Get clarification if necessary. In order to be prepared you have to know the expectations.

I SAID SOAR
The Confidence Talk

Second: What are your strengths and how can your known strengths help with being prepared? Write below something you do very well and how it can help with a primary expectation at work.

Think of a time when being better prepared would have made a difference in your confidence level. What did you do then and what would you do differently to be better prepared in a similar scenario? Focus only on factors that are under your control.

What is one thing you can do to be better prepared at work? One factor that was in my control was allowing myself more preparation time before a meeting or presentation – the result was better content, and better mastery of the content. *Example: getting to know your audience members outside of the meeting room for better relationships and better understanding of your audience.*

I SAID SOAR
The Confidence Talk

There were times when despite having prepared for the presentation, I was still caught off guard by a question or request for new information. When you are not feeling confident, small incidents tend to have a bigger impact than they ordinarily would.

Think of a time when you felt adequately prepared and still encountered challenges and your confidence was negatively affected. Consider why your confidence was still impacted. Was it an unexpected question? Not having a great response? How did you respond then and what would you do differently given the opportunity now? Focus on what is in your control when thinking of what you would do.

> List below steps that you can take to maintain your confidence and perspective even when something unexpected comes up.
> *Example: Pause, breathe, and think before giving a response.*
> *Pause and ask a question that gives you more information. For example "What do you have in mind?"*

Impart

Share your skills, talents, and Knowledge with a diverse audience.

 Impart: to communicate the knowledge of something; to give, convey, or grant from a source.

Impart is about sharing your skills, knowledge, and talent with different audiences. To impart, first review and take stock of your skills and abilities and then share them with others in your organization and professional circles. It is important to track your success and accomplishments, and it is important that your identity is not only tied to your success at your job or only one aspect of your life.

I SAID SOAR
The Confidence Talk

These are the four components I used for tracking and sharing:

- **Recall:** Revisit and read previous projects, notes, articles, and reviews to keep that knowledge fresh
- **Record:** Write it down and make it accessible - Resume, notebook, articles. Share it – in industry and online. I recommend using social media or any current sharing applications, for professional/work sharing.
- **Reach beyond the routine:** Use your skills beyond your daily work. Go beyond your immediate work circle. This will put your skill, talent, knowledge in front of a variety of customers/clients both internal and external to your organization.
- **Relationships:** Maintain your strong positive professional relationships and let your supporters know your professional interests and goals. Your champions will serve as your network and connection to opportunities that match your skills and interests.

Here's what impart looked like for me: I reviewed, then updated my resume. I also reviewed past projects, notes, and even presentations that I had completed or led. Some of my accomplishments had somehow faded from my memory and recalling them served as a booster to my confidence and a reminder of some skills I had not used in a while. Next, I reached out to people I knew in the organization to share with them my interest in other aspects of the work in the organization. In addition to the people I interacted with regularly in the course of work, I was getting to know others in the organization that I would not necessarily have met otherwise. I was also learning more about the organization and gaining a broader view of the work being done. It would be a few more years before I formalized a mentor relationship, and while I did not start with a formal mentor structure, I had access to excellent role models and thought partners.

I SAID SOAR
The Confidence Talk

Diversifying my work and interactions served to build my confidence in the work place and broadened my exposure within the organization. What's more, I was getting to meet and partner with a variety of people at all levels of the organization. I made some long-lasting connections in the course of reaching beyond routine work responsibilities. I was adding to my skills while also having a decidedly improved work experience. I also went beyond the organization – more of that in the chapter on *offering*. Certain aspects of the workplace still required change but those aspects were no longer as consuming as they had been. Essentially my professional experience and identity were no longer limited to my role/title in the organization.

Key Confidence Point:

You are more than any one identity or label and that helps to keep you grounded. Similarly, your professional identity should not be tied to one role, job title, or organization so that your own sense of identity does not become limited to the one.

Applying Impart:

Write down your skills, recent accomplishments, awards and recognitions. Summarize these for any upcoming evaluation or assessment. Review and update your resume to include major accomplishments. Join committees and groups of interest within your organization, in your community, and in your professional arena. For the more introverted among us, focus on building those relationships one person at a time. Quality is more important than quantity.

I SAID SOAR
The Confidence Talk

List your accomplishments, skills, and recognition/awards.
(Don't be bashful in this section. Use the pages on the back if you need more space):

Building on deliverables at work, what is your most important deliverable at work or in your business? There may be more than one but not all carry equal weight. Which of your skills are on display in the process of delivering on this result and who is your audience for this deliverable?

List here those skills you have that are on display or should be seen in the course of your conducting your work or business.

Begin now to build your professional network if you have not already. My professional network is also a personal network. I know some incredible people that are doing impactful and powerful work in their community and beyond. I just so happen to have met them first in a professional setting. How will you go about building your network?

I SAID SOAR
The Confidence Talk

> How will you build your professional network? Write your next steps to growing your network here. Examples: Sign up for a reputable local leadership program, attend your business chamber's events.

Look into opportunities to learn more about the organization or industry beyond your current work circle. Are there any other areas of interest you have in the organization? Are there any barriers to going beyond your current work circle? List any barriers and specific actions that you will take to get the result that is important to you now.

List here the actions to be taken to get to know your organization and professional circles.

Barrier	Action
Example: Not familiar with what else is out there in the organization/industry	*Subscribe to or join the local or national professional group representing that field of interest*

Next let's go through the steps of creating a professional bio. In preparing your bio, you have the opportunity to tell your story and put together a broader profile of who you are and what you do.

I SAID SOAR
The Confidence Talk

Writing your bio (Brief biography for a speaker, panelist, or presenter):

If you have not yet had an opportunity to create or update your bio, use the space below to put together your bio - or elements of a bio. Prepare a bio as though you will be introduced to an audience as part of a panel talking about a subject that is important to you. Your bio is usually a better representation of you than a resume because it incorporates elements of your professional life, personal life, accomplishments, passion, and sometimes dreams. It goes beyond skills to a more rounded picture of you.

Elements of a professional bio:

- Your name, current role, and summary of relevant experience
- Company name and previous role – add these as you deem them fit for the event
- 2 – 3 achievements
- Your passion, goals and aspirations
- 1 – 2 interesting facts about you

Use the space below to note elements of your speaker bio.

Speaker or panelist bio

I SAID SOAR
The Confidence Talk

| |
| |
| |
| |

Include an updated headshot or picture you like in your bio to get it ready to share when needed.

D Don't spread your panic.
My take on 'Fake it till you make it'

They say, "Fake it till you make it" I say, "Don't spread your panic."

At some point in our careers, we have probably all heard the advice to fake it till you make it. I know I was given that advice at a pivotal time in my career. Perhaps it's a phrase that has been popularized in the United States. And yet that advice never quite resonated with me. I adopted an approach that felt more authentic and was more like me, *Don't spread your panic*. That is to say, Pause, assess, then act.

Don't spread your panic probably resonated more with me because I was rejecting the notion of being insincere. The idea of faking it also seemed to go along with the growing culture of people in leadership positions not being able to admit that they did not know something. It also implied for me that you had to pretend in order to be successful and accepted as a leader.

I first started actively practicing *Don't spread your panic* when I realized that I was verbally expressing self-doubt with increasing frequency. This was usually when I was first presented with a daunting new task. At this point in my career, I had most likely already handled something of similar complexity, but the

I SAID SOAR
The Confidence Talk

uncertainty I was experiencing had changed my reaction to new challenges. In response, I started the habit of taking a pause so as not to spread my panic. Taking the pause gave me a moment to gather my thoughts and assess the task at hand.

Whenever I felt a rush of emotion when presented with a challenge – a new project, a new problem, a frustrated customer – I first paused. Don't spread your panic. I would take a few moments to assess and then start to formulate my response. The pause – sometimes as little as 10 seconds – was enough to determine what I wanted my response to be. What started out as daunting was often less so after the pause. If necessary, I would step away from the urgency – put some time and distance between me and the problem - if needed to gather my thoughts.

Adopting *Don't spread your panic* helped to shape my communication and message, in time I found it also helped me avoid absorbing other people's panic.

Don't spread your panic became my advice to myself and later to others. Pause. Give yourself a moment to allow your skills, experience, intuition, and even emotions to be part of your assessment before you respond. This is not about pretending to know it all. It's not about taking on more than you should. After your assessment, you may very well still come to the conclusion that it is indeed too much but with more clarity about what it would take to get it done. Pause, assess, and then decide and share your chosen course of action.

Key Confidence Point:

Don't spread your panic. More often than not, the panic will pass and you will retain your perspective. Give yourself a moment to assess what is in front of you.

I SAID SOAR
The Confidence Talk

Applying Don't Spread Your Panic:

What does *Don't spread you panic* look like for you in your work environment?

Describe your initial reaction(s) when you are faced with a daunting task or a work situation that causes a rush of emotions – fear, panic, worry, etc. What do you tell yourself? What do you tell others? *(Any specific example can be used here.)*

I SAID SOAR
The Confidence Talk

Summarize below at least one example where your skill helped with a new daunting task, or where your ability evolved to be different from the initial reaction you had to a new, daunting task.

Initial Reaction to a New, Daunting Task

The reality of your skill/ability

List ways that you avoid spreading your panic and what helps with gaining perspective on intimidating tasks.

I SAID SOAR
The Confidence Talk

Don't spread your panic. Pause, assess, and then decide how you want to proceed. You've got this. You know things today that you did not know even a few months ago. You have done things today that you had not done five years ago. You are evolving, and you continue to learn and grow. So, the next time you feel that surge of emotion you don't have to fake it, you've already made it.

The BONUS section

I SAID SOAR
The Confidence Talk

The BONUS section

Let's go over two bonus points before we get into SOAR. The first bonus point is *People are people* and the second one is *It's not you, and it's not just you.*

Here are two quotes and two guiding principles to help keep things in perspective:

> When people show you who they are, believe them the first time.
>
> **MAYA ANGELOU**

> A large chair does not make a king.
>
> **SUDANESE PROVERB**

💡 It just may not be personal; people have their own stuff including self-doubt and low self esteem.

💡 There's no need to absorb another person's doubt about your ability.

I SAID SOAR
The Confidence Talk

Bonus 1: People are People

There are some things that affect and influence people that have absolutely nothing to do with you. In the workplace we call it office politics, but it's just people being people. Same as elementary school, secondary school, and all stages of life – we are merely human. Having an important title does not make a person everything you expect from that title. It is the person that matters and you may just be the most grounded and self-assured person in the room. This is an important reality to keep in mind. People are people. This does not excuse discourtesy or mean that your role becomes one of accommodating inappropriate behavior; this is only to say that the behavior a person demonstrates is often more about them than it is about you. So, assign the behavior its proper place. If you are not yet adept at doing so, keep practicing.

Imagine driving along the road when someone in another car suddenly cuts in front of you forcing you to step on the brakes immediately to avoid a collision with their car.

Let's say that once you recover from the sudden stop that you are indignant. After all, how dare they force you to suddenly stop, make a split-second decision about whether you can safely change lanes, and not to mention the increased heart rate that came along with the sudden stop? They did that and then carried on driving. What do you do? Do you immediately speed up, look ahead to get them in your sights, honk your car horn, change lanes in hopes of catching up with them to give them a piece of your mind?

If you had a way of knowing the perspective of the driver of the other vehicle, would that change how you feel or how you react?

I SAID SOAR
The Confidence Talk

Let's look at some possible scenarios:

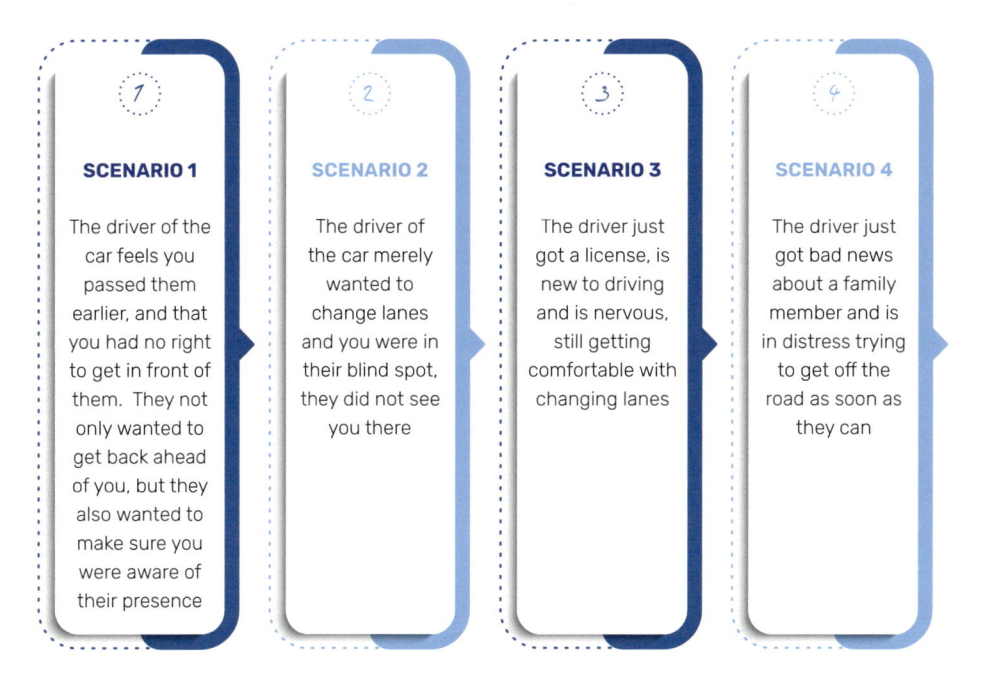

SCENARIO 1	SCENARIO 2	SCENARIO 3	SCENARIO 4
The driver of the car feels you passed them earlier, and that you had no right to get in front of them. They not only wanted to get back ahead of you, but they also wanted to make sure you were aware of their presence	The driver of the car merely wanted to change lanes and you were in their blind spot, they did not see you there	The driver just got a license, is new to driving and is nervous, still getting comfortable with changing lanes	The driver just got bad news about a family member and is in distress trying to get off the road as soon as they can

You may respond differently knowing the various scenarios. Regardless of that driver's story, you have been forced to suddenly slow down, maybe even change lanes to be safe. So, what do you do?

The bigger question here is this: where were you going before you encountered this other car and driver? Lest you be taken off course and away from your destination, consider in responding if it is worth changing your goal or timeline to focus on this incident.

People are just people after all is said and done and they have their own stuff. Before you change you lane and pace solely out of reaction, check on yourself. Take stock of what's around you and assign it its proper place so that you do not relinquish your own plans.

I SAID SOAR
The Confidence Talk

Bonus 2: It's not you and it's not just you

This is the validation station. Are you going through a difficult time at work? Do you find that even with a "big" title and responsibility your confidence has waned? I'm here to tell you it's not you and it's not just you. Until more recent years, there has been more emphasis on imposter syndrome and not as much on the impact of the work environment on people who arrived in the workforce perfectly capable and confident in their abilities. Over time, having been steeped in an environment of doubt you started to experience what I call "acquired imposter syndrome". You did not come in with self doubt but you likely absorbed it from the prevailing culture.

Keep this bonus message in mind while you continue to do the amazing things you do. You see, the feeling and consciousness of your own power is enough to change the outcome of a situation and that's what I want you to retain. I want to you to go into situations without being unduly anxious or worried about it, I want you to be able to walk into work situations with your shoulders relaxed, head held high, free to focus on the work. I want you to continue to bask in the knowledge and feeling of your power, influence, gratitude, and confidence in the untainted state in which it exists. Focus on you and your purpose.

What are the experiences that can impact your confidence over time? Perhaps you hear positive comments about your work but do not see a matching promotion or raise? Or you may have people wonder about your ability to be successful after you have already demonstrated you can handle more. Have you started to wonder if it's you? **It's not you and it's not just you**. When I started to work on reclaiming my confidence, I realized that I had previously encountered many scenarios that could have impacted my confidence, but I had a different perspective at the time of these encounters and did not recognize them for what they were. I will give you an example.

I SAID SOAR
The Confidence Talk

The first time I became aware of a person questioning my role in a leadership position, my confidence was intact. At the time, my perspective on their questioning my being in the role I had was the following:

1. It's not personal as they don't know me yet
2. It is their opinion, it's not a reflection of me
3. My work speaks for itself (we have already covered this in *Impart*)
4. They will learn what I do
5. They will come to like having me in this role

Most of this was true, but I had no evidence that the last two did happen. If I had encountered this reality when my confidence was low, I would have suffered a crisis of confidence and probably more significant impact to my career. My perspective was rooted in my self-confidence, but I also incorrectly assumed best intentions. It turned out that the questioning was not based on knowing anything about me or my work. Rather it was based on an unfounded decision of who they thought I might be. Also known as bias. While at the time it seemed like a situation unique to me, it was not. I have had conversations with many people – mostly women – about confidence and what affects their confidence at work. And more often than not, the culprit has been bias. Bias is a human reality; it is also people being people. It is to be expected. What matters in the workplace is whether that bias is acknowledged, addressed, and its impact mitigated. The other major factor for the workplace is competence in leadership training. Confidence and competence in a safe environment make for a winning formula. That's a subject for another talk: Confidence and Competence within a culture of Psychological safety and continuous improvement makes for a thriving work environment. The impact of unchecked bias can be detrimental to the individual and costly to the organization – financially and socially. A psychologically safe environment that is inclusive and retains the ability to adapt to change yields in dividends. But well before you may have been aware of a study, you had probably seen or experienced bias whether you were conscious of it or not.

I SAID SOAR
The Confidence Talk

My goal in mentioning this is to validate the feelings that you may have had that something is off. More importantly, it is to identify and name it so that you can decide what you can do to maintain or reclaim your confidence. Sometimes these biased actions are unintentional and other times they are not. Similar to the analogy of being cut off when driving, whether intentional or not, it still affected you.

In talking with various people about their careers and confidence I found that there were a lot of similar experiences. Often about mid-career, after a stretch of doing the same thing, there was a sense that their career was stalling. There was a shift in their workplace experience. They had performed well, often exceeding expectations and yet - seemingly inexplicably - they were no longer being recognized or promoted for their work. They found themselves either frustrated, exhausted, or both. When they advocated for themselves based on demonstrated ability, their ambition was met with disregard or discouragement sometimes followed by varying degrees of criticism. Often times, a gatekeeper of advancement in the organization – such as a direct manager – seemed to take their professional drive and aptitude as a personal affront and responded accordingly. In some instances, it showed as a negative performance assessment, in other instances it was a negative campaign within the organization. A negative campaign would look like an attempt to undermine the individual by speaking poorly about the person in multiple work circles to discredit them.

Some experiences were not as direct. Instead, the response received was shrouded in supportive explanations for why they may not want the promotion or did not qualify for the promotion this time. It may sound like, "you're doing such a good job, keep this up and I am sure you will be promoted next". Except the next time continues to be deferred.

Another version is receiving advice about advancing that does not appear to be necessary for counterparts who are advancing in the organization. When these observed outcomes are questioned, those questions are met with anything from incredulity to indignation. This is the kind of mixed messaging that can cause the dissonance I described earlier in the book – something doesn't quite make sense or seem right. Don't ignore the dissonance. It's not you, and it's not just you.

The main idea here is to recognize and acknowledge when there is a change in you or around you. Do not ignore your instincts or experience, rather face the sentiment and decide how best to address the change. Start by identifying what you need, then take a step back to identify patterns and opportunities. If any of the experiences in this book are familiar because something similar has happened to you or someone you know, it is more of an indication of opportunities to improve systems within the organization.

A lot has changed since I first wrote notes for what was to become The Confidence Talk©. The most notable change was a global one - the world experienced the Covid-19 pandemic. The pandemic, and all that came with it, challenged and changed our lives in so many ways. In the workplace, the way that people work, meet, and engage was changed in a major way. With the pandemic as the backdrop, conversations about the work environment, working remotely, isolation, burnout, and belonging became commonplace. The focus on the workplace popularized conversations about equity, inclusion, belonging, and the impact of bias on people in the workplace. None of it was new, but there was a renewed focus on what was already an issue for so many in the workplace and that is the underpinning for this section.

There are still opportunities for organizations to be intentional in minimizing the impact of bias on their employees at all levels of the organization. This may include creating learning opportunities to recognize and address bias, investigating patterns with turnover, and creating tools to minimize the impact of bias on evaluations and the advancement processes. If you are a leader or in a position to influence decision makers in an organization, you are in a position to implement or support systematic changes.

I SAID SOAR
The Confidence Talk

As you advance and grow your circle of influence, put in place processes that will minimize the impact of bias on people in your organization. Share your story and serve as a mentor and supporter to others who have gone through similar situations. If you have not personally experienced any of this, you can still be a part of helping another person reclaim their confidence. It also helps to be in charge so if you are not already, consider becoming the boss but remember to be the change you want to see. Be part of the change you want to see both in the experience of the people and in the success of your organization.

In the note pages that follow this section, write down where the messages in this bonus section may apply to your experiences. Also note any change around you, what the change signals to you, your desired outcome and next steps.

Notes:

Notes:

Notes:

Part - 2

Confidence IN You

I SAID SOAR
The Confidence Talk

> Number one in your life's blueprint, should be a deep belief in your own dignity, your worth and your own somebodiness.
>
> **DR. MARTIN LUTHER KING JR.**

The Confidence IN You

Here we turn the focus to internal confidence. This is about feeling confident, knowing who you are, and knowing that you are capable beyond what you do at work. Here you get to focus on your identity and sense of self beyond your job title or work identity. This is about having access to the belief that you can do what needs to be done and that you will pull through - even when your feelings waver. Part 2 is SOAR – the confidence in you. We turn inward and look at reclaiming self-confidence with Self-regard, Offering, Advance, and Recharge/Refuel.

Self-Regard
Know yourself. Like yourself.

> Self-regard: regard for or consideration of oneself or one's own interests.

Regard means respect and can also mean concern; consideration implies concern and respect but also means understanding. So, self-regard can also be described as having respect, understanding, and consideration of yourself and your own interests. Sometimes out of respect and concern for others we allow our self-regard to take a backseat. Leading and supporting others often means striking a balance between what your team needs to be successful and how best to support the organizational goals. This can easily evolve into leaving yourself out of the equation in a bid to be what the team needs. In my case, I was minimizing my assessment of some situations. In the process of reserving my opinion in hopes of achieving harmony around me, I inadvertently created disharmony within me. I was drifting away from authenticity and as a result not feeling grounded. I had to take a step back to answer questions like these for myself:

- Who am I?
- Am I myself at work?
- What am I here to do?
- Am I doing what I came here to do?

This introspection ended up being similar to the skills cataloging that I had done for my resume, but this was for me. In answering the questions, I was reminded of my background, my values, the way I chose to work with people, why I work the way I do, and what I had accomplished with my personal style. It was also accepting myself again – no right or wrong, no overthinking - just getting to know myself. Getting re-familiarized with myself in an intentional way gave me a greater sense of control. It also allowed me to tap into my instincts once again. I could more confidently draw on my experiences and benefit from my intuition because I was not second-guessing myself.

This notion of first understanding myself reminds me of training I went through as a cashier many years ago – a story I sometimes share. There was a trainer, a former law enforcement officer, who was brought in to teach the new cashiers about identifying counterfeit bills. As you can imagine, any business accepting cash would want to avoid fake money, so it was worth investing in this training. And in case cash is out of style and perhaps not in existence when you read this, cash is (or was) paper money and was at some point the most common form of legal tender for transactions. Back to the training story – while we were shown some of the latest types of counterfeit dollar bills, the trainer's real strategy and message to us was this: get to know the real dollar bill very, very well. Know the real thing.

I SAID SOAR
The Confidence Talk

If you know the real thing, you are less likely to be deceived by a fake bill. In getting to know myself, I did not necessarily have to know a person's intentions, their personality, or position. What I knew was what I liked, what I didn't like, my biases, and how I respond under certain circumstances. I could recognize my own response to a person's action – or inaction.

One of the main outcomes of respecting myself is setting boundaries and creating awareness of those boundaries if they are crossed. This was particularly important in the work setting where work would require ongoing interactions and collaboration. Having to make someone aware that they had crossed a boundary or had acted inappropriately was not a common occurrence. But when it did happen, creating awareness really meant letting the person know that they had crossed the boundary in such a way that they had an opportunity to share their perspective. Most of the time it was an unintentional slight – an apology, a new understanding, and back to work. I have included two examples in response to the questions about boundaries at the end of this chapter.

Getting to know myself very well made me less reactive, it made me a better leader, a better colleague, and it afforded me more moments of calm. I was reminded that coming from a place of self-regard and liking myself was both a positive and a powerful approach to any interaction.

So, who are you? Ask yourself this question then ponder your responses. Reconnect to your motivations, dreams, fears, vulnerability, hopes, and your power – especially if you have fallen into the habit of minimizing yourself. This is like an internal *Suit up*. Stand tall within yourself.

I SAID SOAR
The Confidence Talk

Key Confidence Point:

Show respect and consideration for yourself. Know yourself and like yourself. You are what makes *it* happen.

Applying Self-regard:

Who are you? Heritage, background, life experiences, beliefs, character, values, etc.

What are some things that are special or different about you? Include who you are, what you can do - abilities, passions, hobbies, and strengths including those you may not use at work.

I SAID SOAR
The Confidence Talk

What can easily get you annoyed or angry, and how do you deal with it?

What boundaries have you set or do you need to set? How will you set those boundaries moving forward? How will you create awareness if needed?
Examples for creating awareness:
"It may not have been your intention to (fill in the effect/impact of their action) but that is what happened when you (fill in the action)"
"That's not ok with me".

I SAID SOAR
The Confidence Talk

What do you like about yourself and what have others said that they like about you?

What do you care about? What would you work on for free?

O

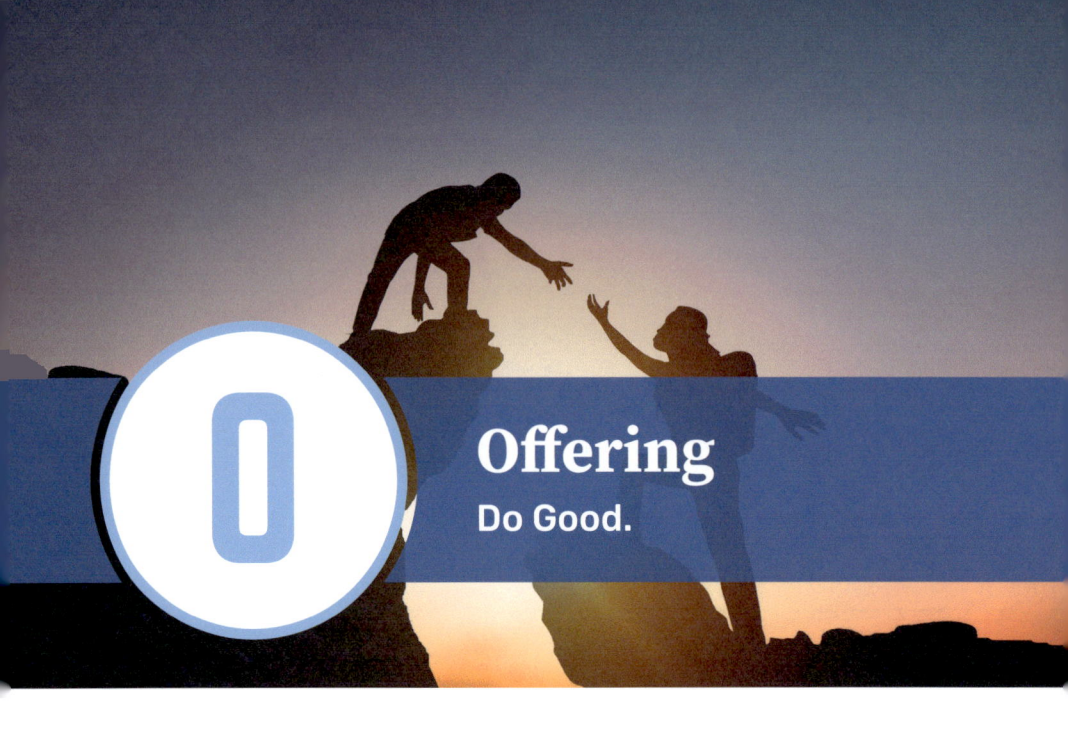

Offering
Do Good.

Offering ~ A contribution. Something offered.

The impact of feeling less confident at work was magnified by the fact that my job had become a very big part of my identity. In spending so much time at work and with work, I had not spent nearly enough time doing things that I enjoyed that were not tied to my job and my work identity. I resolved to get involved in the community. This entailed going beyond my usual routine to engage with non-profits and other volunteer opportunities. I helped out in the library, took courses, learned about my community through a local leadership organization and started looking into joining nonprofit boards. Soon I was directly involved in doing good around me beyond work. I used my skills and abilities to help

I SAID SOAR
The Confidence Talk

others and, in the process, broadened my focus. I found that I could join a board meeting at the end of a long workday and feel energized about the good being done in the community. Being involved in the community also created opportunities to meet others in the community. This non-work, non-home activity started out as an extension of my professional identity and evolved to become more personal and fulfilling.

Offering is about contributing in ways that are also meaningful to you. You use your skills or talents and support the community or people around you in areas that are near and dear to your heart. Offering is about investing in others but it is also an investment in yourself. One example of how doing good for others is doing good for yourself is serving as a mentor. Anyone who serves as a mentor will tell you they learn from the person they are mentoring as well. Being involved in the community gave me an opportunity to mentor and learn from incredible leaders in the community. I found myself inspired by the leaders I encountered and energized by the collaborations and connections I was making. Here too my focus was no longer only on my identity at work. Offering put some distance between me and the challenges I was experiencing, allowing me to gain a different perspective. The bonus was that in the process, I was adding value and being a part of positive change in my community. This proved to be more rewarding than I anticipated. Doing good did me good.

Key Confidence Point:

Do good. Step out and be a part of building the community. Be a part of something, bigger than you, that is outside of your work expectations.

I SAID SOAR
The Confidence Talk

Applying Offering:

Who around you could benefit from your using your natural abilities, passion, and skills? Which organizations can you support in your community, in the world? Give or participate in areas that are meaningful to you. Be a part of another person's success story.

Community and Causes:

List below any local nonprofit/charitable organizations or programs that you are interested in supporting or already supporting. Include causes that are of interest or important to you (Art, health, food insecurity/hunger, homelessness, leadership, literacy, women's health/interest, science, etc.). Decide which one(s) you want to start working with and reach out to establish how you can help and a date to begin helping.

Organization or Cause	Available activities	Contact info/date

A

Advance
Keep Training.

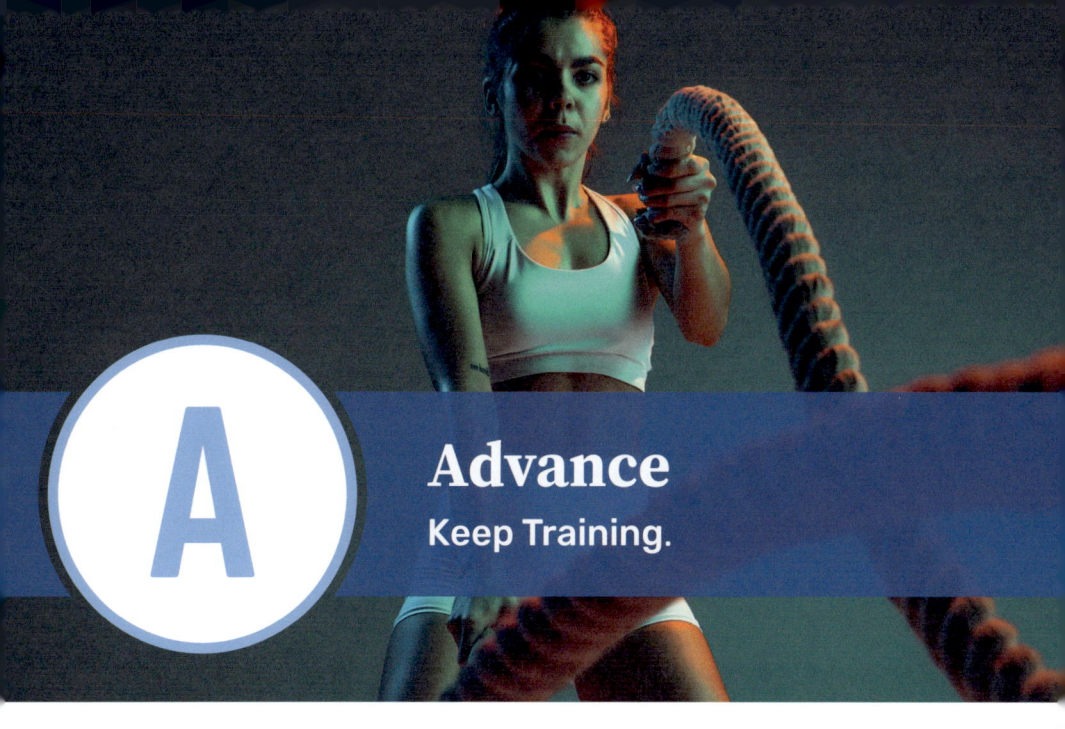

Advance: Move forward in a purposeful way. Make progress.

Advance means keep your eye on the prize. Keep working towards your goals. Keep training and keep learning.

This lesson came from being absorbed by work. We had a saying growing up, "Variety is the spice of life". Diversifying my work experience in the community was helpful in adding to the variety, the spice of my work life. The internal parallel for me was to remember my broader goals – both career and personal.

Being absorbed by work also had the effect of my defining my progress and success almost entirely in the terms of the organizational ladder. Wins were great, but disappointments were also great. Disappointments at work had

I SAID SOAR
The Confidence Talk

a larger impact than they would ordinarily have had on me. I was also more easily drawn into negative dynamics and a negative outlook. . It was time to pay attention to broader personal and professional development. To resume training in a matter of speaking.

An analogy I often use in talking about *Advance* is that of an Olympic athlete who plans to return to the Olympics. That event is four years out and yet will dictate many decisions the athlete makes and possibly even the company she keeps. No matter what else she is working on in the interim, that goal of returning to the Olympics remains the driving force behind her activities. To return, she cannot be complacent or distracted. She would practice, train, and remain focused on that goal.

Taking a step back from the immediate to look at the big picture allowed me to focus on my intentions and, indirectly, on my wellbeing Simply looking at goals I experienced an increased sense of satisfaction and accomplishment. This reminds me of a driving lesson I learned early on as a student driver.

When I was learning to drive, I was very nervous about driving on the freeway and specifically avoided the fast lane. A friend who was teaching me to drive encouraged me to move to the fast lane as the next step of my practice. I told him I was nervous about the fast lane because I was afraid that I would hit the median wall that separated the opposing lanes of traffic. His advice was simple, focus on where you're going and where you want to be, not where you don't want to be. Keep your eyes on the road, and not on the median wall. The work equivalent was that I was losing sight of my big picture and had taken my eyes off the big picture which included broader goals. Making progress towards my goals helped to recalibrate my focus I still use Advance when I need to refocus on my goals or my reason for stepping into a role.

What are you working towards? What is your goal? These were questions I had to ask myself when I realized I was frequently focused on what was wrong and what I didn't want. While there was plenty to do, and the work filled the days, I

I SAID SOAR
The Confidence Talk

had completely shelved my goals. Losing sight of my goal allowed more trivial aspects of the work to seem larger than they were and to negatively impact my sense of purpose. First, I needed to pause and take stock of what I was doing and what I wanted to.

Advance translated to looking beyond only organizational goals to my personal and professional goals. I revisited my long-term goals. I also resumed attending educational events that were arranged by industry experts and started looking into academic programs in my areas of interest. Here again I gained perspective on a more personal level.

Key Confidence Point:

Keep your eyes on the prize. Do not lose sight of your aspirations. Invest in your development and wellbeing.

Applying Advance:

- What is your biggest goal?
- What did you set out to do and what is your why?
- What are your immediate/short term goals?
- What action(s) have you taken towards these goals?
- What additional actions can you take towards these goals?

I SAID SOAR
The Confidence Talk

Short Term Goal(s):

> List tasks and schedule dates for completion of tasks related to this goal. These do not have to be work related. Select a method for follow up that will lead to success – use a deadline, accountability partner, reward, etc.

Big Picture/Longer Term Goal:

> List activities, tasks, and smaller goals that support this bigger goal.

I SAID SOAR
The Confidence Talk

What is something you can do today or this week that is related to your goals?
Example: Research certificate programs, sign up for an event or program by a professional organization.

R

Recharge/Refuel
At the village or At the pump

Recharge: Restore, revitalize. To revive or restore energy, stamina, enthusiasm, etc.

Refuel: To take on a fresh supply of fuel. To supply or be supplied with fresh fuel.

Your Village:

This refers to safe spaces where can you rest, be vulnerable if necessary, and be reminded of who you are, where you come from, where you are going, and what you are capable of doing.

I SAID SOAR
The Confidence Talk

The Pump:

This refers to formal, trained sources of restoration. Therapist (massage, physical, occupational), psychologist, faith leader, mentor, etc.

There is rest, and there is revitalization. Recharge/Refuel means taking the time to restore your energy, stamina, and enthusiasm. Part of rebuilding confidence is to give yourself an opportunity to recover sufficiently physically, mentally, and any other way that is needed. Recharging/refueling refers to getting your power level up again. In addition to resting, part of replenishing is to take care of your overall wellbeing. You cannot sustain taking care of yourself and others when you are running low on energy and stamina yourself.

In addition to a growing sense of uncertainty, at a point in all of this, I was not sleeping well. It was a busy time to be sure but that not the main thing that kept work on my mind. You see, direct, work-related, quantifiable problems – now that I could do. But that was not the challenge. Remember, I had been silent and accepting. Accepting without question was not working for me. But I stayed with it for a while and the uncertainty swelled. I was not being myself and it was taking a toll on my disposition and my sleep.

I needed a safe space to process what I was experiencing. A space where I could talk through what was impacting me. Over time as I got back into the habit of setting boundaries and addressing any unresolved issues, I was able to rest easier. But until then, I needed a safe place to think through and address the various aspects of work that had been impacting me. I took the time to reach out to trusted friends and loved ones. This act of resting and recovering in community is what I refer to as recharge/refuel. My village was home figuratively and literally.

Spending time with family and friends served as a reminder of who I am, where I have come from, and where I want to go. Often with love and laughter my parents and siblings would reference attitudes and preferences I have had from childhood. Childhood friends would describe the version of me they had seen

I SAID SOAR
The Confidence Talk

and grown up with - even as we talked about the present. I actively sought out my connection to home, to feeling grounded, to being around people who wished me well as I took the time to sort myself out.

I had the advantage of a supportive family unit. While I was sorting myself out at work, home was stable. I knew that when leaving for work in the morning and returning in the evening. Home was the constant and that was part of my confidence. Family helped me maintain perspective.

When it was a stressful time at work, recharging was that much more important. I started identifying ways to schedule time for things I enjoyed. I considered incorporating exercise into my week and decided to start with dancing at home. I also took walks with friends, looked for a relatively inexpensive massage therapy option, and carved out some time to read.

Rest. Recharge. Refuel. It may just be time to go home – figuratively speaking. Going home to your village, to where people know you and your power. Spend time at home with those who recognize your ability and are happy to share reminders and memories of what you are capable of. Go to a place where you have the time and space to pause, reflect, and gather yourself. This is your village - your friends and family who can function as mirrors holding positive reflections of you that you may have let go of, or forgotten.

If you do not have family or friends who can serve in this role, or you cannot go "home", you can recharge or refuel at the "pump". Choose a formal or professional resource that will serve as a sounding board, a supporter, and a guide. Someone who can also serve as a reminder of your strengths and abilities. This may be any combination of a mentor and guide at work, a mentor through a leadership program, a therapist for mental health check ins, and a physical therapist or massage therapist to address physical self-care. There is a better appreciation and awareness of the need for mental health care. Even with a supportive village, to truly recharge, you may need the support of a qualified mental health professional.

I SAID SOAR
The Confidence Talk

This next part may go without saying, but we all need to rest. We need to recuperate from the impact of the day.

This includes all the basics – food, water, and rest. We also need to recharge or refuel, to keep going. As challenging as work can be, it's not everything and there is a lot to be grateful for in life. However, when you are in the thick of things, you may forget. You may forget to reach out to your community, to take stock of your own self. Hence the reminder to rest, recharge, and renew your focus.

> **Key Confidence Point:**
> Take care of yourself and make the most of this life. Practice caring for yourself in meaningful ways. The better you are, the better you will do.

Applying Recharge/Refuel:

What can you do, or should you be doing to recharge? What are the activities that energize you? What are the activities that replenish you?

I SAID SOAR
The Confidence Talk

Are there activities that you should eliminate or avoid? List them here.

Are there boundaries that you need to set? List here which boundaries and how you can begin to set them.

Who? What? Where is your village and/or pump?

I SAID SOAR
The Confidence Talk

Write below what steps you will take to recharge or refuel.

Conclusion

I SAID SOAR
The Confidence Talk

That is The Confidence Talk.

Now that we have had this talk, what stood out the most for you? What elements have you already started applying?

There is space on the next few pages for you to elaborate on what has resonated the most with you in this book. Write it down so that you do not forget it and so that you can revisit it later when you pick up this book again.

You may not need all these strategies at once, and you may need them more than once. Pick what works for you and use it as often as needed. Incorporate them into your style and pace to make it organic. Make it yours.

Here's one more reminder of I SAID SOAR, The Confidence talk©.

The Confidence on you: S.A.I.D.	**The Confidence in you: S.O.A.R.**
▸ Suit up	▸ Self-regard
▸ Always prepared	▸ Offering
▸ Impart	▸ Advance
▸ Don't spread your panic	▸ Recharge/Refuel

Now that you have gone through these strategies and reminders, what actions will you take to further build your self-confidence? What steps will you take that you may have shied away from previously?

Whichever strategies you adopt, remember to use all the tools at your disposal. Be still. Pray. Sing. Meditate. Bury your feet in the sand. Put your face to the sun. Listen to the breeze in the trees or the sounds of a river. Breathe. Soar.

Here's to you.

Cheers,

Idara

Notes:

Notes:

Notes:

Notes:

Notes:

Notes:

IDARA INWEK OGUNSAJU

Idara Inwek Ogunsaju is the founder of The Antorge Group, LLC a Change Management and Confidence consulting practice. The Antorge Group focuses on building confidence in women in the workplace and supports organizations in creating spaces that embrace confident women.

I first created The Confidence Talk© as a talk with a reminder to "Be still". The talk is the story of observations and strategies I applied in a work setting to reclaim the power and confidence that I had lost in that phase of my career. It evolved from a talk to a book. I SAID SOAR, is an acronym for the strategies to use for reclaiming your confidence. With the workplace as the backdrop for the strategies, The Confidence Talk© covers showing confidence as well as feeling confident in the workplace. It also covers the impact the work environment can have on one's confidence. In the book you will also find a bonus section and space for notes as you go through these strategies.

Additional Credits:
Book Cover design: Pandora_Halk
Book layout and internal design: Abdul Rehman
Image, Introduction: Jennie Edwards, Guided by Imagination
Image, Conclusion: Brothers Scope Media

I SAID SOAR
The Confidence Talk

Made in the USA
Columbia, SC
21 September 2024